Heroes for Young Readers
ACTIVITY GUIDE
for Books 5–8

Amy Carmichael • Corrie ten Boom
Mary Slessor • William Carey

Renee Taft Meloche

YWAM
PUBLISHING

P.O. BOX 55787 SEATTLE, WA 98155

YWAM Publishing is the publishing ministry of Youth With A Mission. Youth With A Mission (YWAM) is an international missionary organization of Christians from many denominations dedicated to presenting Jesus Christ to this generation. To this end, YWAM has focused its efforts in three main areas: (1) training and equipping believers for their part in fulfilling the Great Commission (Matthew 28:19), (2) personal evangelism, and (3) mercy ministry (medical and relief work).

For a free catalog of books and materials, contact:

YWAM Publishing
P.O. Box 55787, Seattle, WA 98155
(425) 771-1153 or (800) 922-2143
www.ywampublishing.com

Heroes for Young Readers Activity Guide for Books 5–8
Copyright © 2005 by Renee Taft Meloche

10 09 08 07 06 05   10 9 8 7 6 5 4 3 2 1

Published by Youth With A Mission Publishing
P.O. Box 55787
Seattle, WA 98155

ISBN 1-57658-368-6 (10-digit)
ISBN 978-1-57658-368-5 (13-digit)

Printed in the United States of America.

Contents

Introduction

This activity guide is designed to accompany the following books from the Heroes for Young Readers series by Renee Taft Meloche and Bryan Pollard: *Amy Carmichael: Rescuing the Children*; *Corrie ten Boom: Shining in the Darkness*; *Mary Slessor: Courage in Africa*; and *William Carey: Bearer of Good News*. It provides the Christian schoolteacher, Sunday-school teacher, and homeschooling parent with ways to teach and reinforce the important lessons of these books.

Each book contains the following parts:

❖ **Coloring Page.** There is a picture of each hero with memorable people and events surrounding him or her for the children to color.

❖ **Hero Song.** The hero song is a tool to reinforce the main lesson of the hero. Music is often more memorable than spoken or written text.

❖ **Character Quality.** Each hero is given a character quality for the children to focus on. Discussion questions and visual aids are provided.

❖ **Character Activity.** The character activity uses drama or arts and crafts to convey more fully the character quality of the hero.

❖ **Character Song.** The character song encourages children to develop the particular character quality in their own lives.

❖ **Shoebox Activity.** This activity uses arts and crafts to create a keepsake to remember each hero and how they served. The children will put this keepsake into a shoebox (or other container) so that they will have a treasure box of memories of the heroes.

❖ **Cultural Page.** This page illustrates something that is representative of the country each hero worked in as a missionary, such as an animal, game, craft, or recipe.

❖ **Map.** The map page, which the children will color, shows the country or countries the hero lived in growing up and as a missionary.

❖ **Flag.** A flag (usually of the country the hero worked in as a missionary) is provided for the children to color.

❖ **Fact Quiz.** This page tests the children's comprehension of each hero story by giving true and false statements inside a particular object that relates to that story. The children will color in the true statements and draw an X over the false statements.

❖ **Fun with Rhyme.** This page has five stanzas from each hero story. The last word of each stanza is blank, and the children try to fill in the blank, rhyming it with the last word in the second line. A Word Bank is provided for very young readers. (When making copies, the Word Bank can be covered up for the more advanced reader and speller.)

❖ **Crossword Puzzle.** This page tests the children's comprehension of each story. A Word Bank is provided for young readers. (Again, when making copies, the Word Bank can be covered up.)

❖ **Can You Name the Hero?** This exercise has four stanzas, each providing clues about a hero. The children guess which hero each stanza is about.

Before you begin this activity guide, you may want to highlight which activities best suit your needs. For instance, a Sunday-school teacher might want to focus on the coloring pages, songs, character activities, and shoebox activities, while a schoolteacher might want to focus more on the crossword puzzle, fact, map, and cultural pages. A thirteen-week syllabus is included at the end of this activity guide for those parents and teachers who would like a guide to covering some or all of the activities.

Reinforcing stories with fun and creative illustrations, songs, drama, and arts and crafts brings the heroes to life and helps the children remember the important lessons learned through the lives of heroes—ordinary men and women who did extraordinary things with God.

Amy Carmichael: Rescuing the Children

Amy Carmichael Song

Amy went to India and left her home behind. The children there loved Amy since she was so very kind.

In India silk saris were the clothes the rich women wore. But Amy dressed in cotton just exactly like the poor.

In India, in India, she traveled all through India. Though tigers watched her in the night, she felt God's love and light.

In India, in India, she traveled all through India. She took young girls in as her own and gave them a safe home.

The Good Character Quality of Amy Carmichael

Definition of Kindness: Warm-hearted, considerate, and loving.

Bible Verse: "Clothe yourselves with compassion, kindness, humility, gentleness and patience" (Colossians 3:12).

Materials

- ❖ Copy of the crown, strip, and diamond jewel labeled "kindness" on page 12 for each child (use heavy white paper or card stock; if you do not wish to have the children color their crowns, use heavy yellow paper or yellow card stock)
- ❖ Scissors
- ❖ Crayons or colored pencils
- ❖ Stapler
- ❖ Tape or glue

Steps to Follow

1. Introduce the character quality of kindness, which describes Amy, and discuss its meaning with the children. Read aloud the Bible verse above.

2. Have the children color and cut out the diamond labeled "kindness." (Because it is a diamond, tell them they may want to leave the middle part white.)

3. Have the children color and cut out the crown and strip. Read aloud the following Bible verse: "Now there is in store for me the crown of righteousness, which the Lord, the righteous Judge, will award to me on that day" (2 Timothy 4:8).

4. Have the children tape or glue the diamond to the crown. Then have them staple the strip to the crown and put it around their heads. The crowns will serve as their "thinking caps" about kindness.

5. Ask the children, "How did Amy show kindness in her life through her words and actions?"

- ❖ She visited the local slums and passed out bread and Bible stories.
- ❖ She took care of the shawlies and had a large building built for them.
- ❖ She helped the children of India and gave them a safe and loving home to live in.

6. Ask the children if they know someone—a parent, neighbor, or friend—who shows kindness to others in their lives. Have them tell the class about this person.

7. Ask the children to think of ways they can show kindness to others, such as:
   - ❖ Comforting someone who is sad
   - ❖ Visiting someone who is ill or injured
   - ❖ Sharing a special treat with someone
   - ❖ Reading or playing with a younger brother or sister

8. Have the children sing the character song "We'll Show Kindness" on page 13. (This song is sung to the tune of "Do Your Ears Hang Low?" If you have the CD for Amy Carmichael, you can have the children follow or sing along with this song. At the end of the CD, there is a solo piano accompaniment, which the children can sing along with as well.)

Note: This activity carries over into all the hero stories that follow. For each hero, there will be a new character quality inside a different jewel. You can have the children keep adding jewels to the crowns that they've already made or have them make new crowns each time this activity is repeated. Please be aware that the jewels are a fun way to reinforce the lesson, not a suggestion that the children should expect to be rewarded for doing the right thing as Christians.

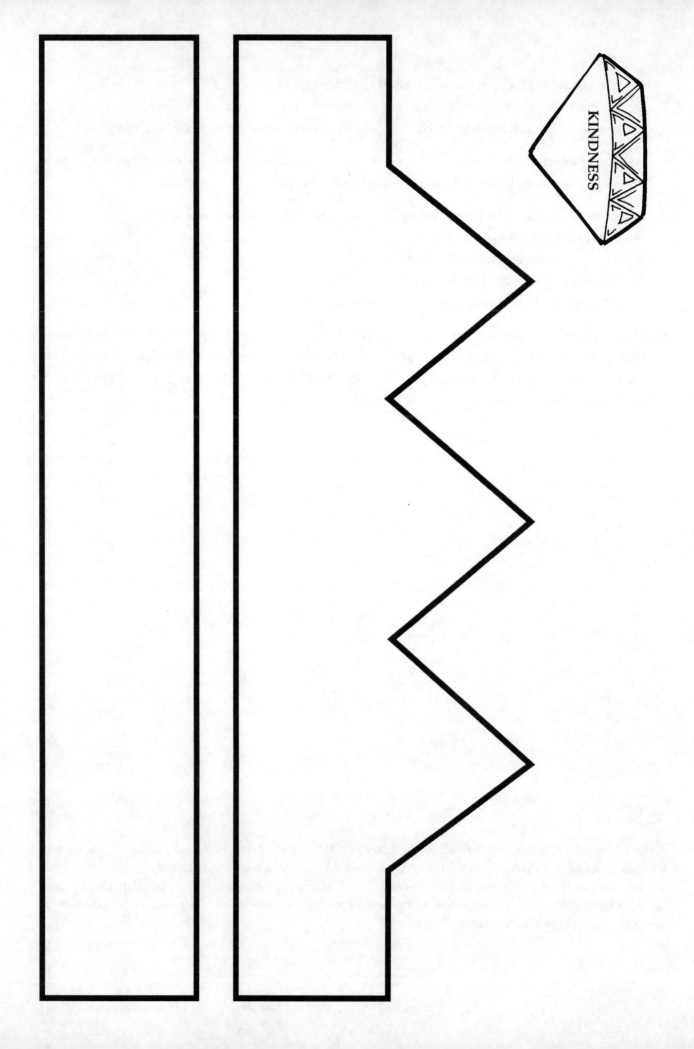

KINDNESS

Amy Carmichael Character Song

We'll Show Kindness

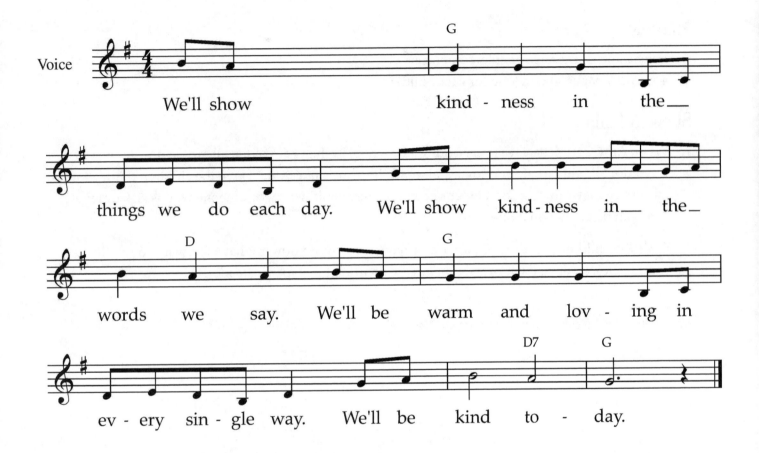

Voice

We'll show kind - ness in the __ things we do each day. We'll show kind - ness in __ the __ words we say. We'll be warm and lov - ing in ev - ery sin - gle way. We'll be kind to - day.

Character Activity for Amy Carmichael

Writing or Drawing a Special Note

Materials

❖ Pencils, pens, crayons, or colored pencils

❖ 4 x 4 inch paper square (one for each child)

Steps to Follow

1. When Amy Carmichael was very young, she wrote, "When I am older, all grown up, I know what I will do; I'll build a safe and loving place for little girls like you." Have the children think about a promise they can make or a letter of comfort they could write to someone who is sick or lonely (this can be an imaginary person).

2. Give the children a square of paper and have them write down what they want to say. If they can't write yet, have them draw a picture or decorate the paper instead.

Note: This activity carries over into the Shoebox Activity on the following page.

Shoebox Activity for Amy Carmichael
Making Special Cards

Note to parents and teachers: A Shoebox Activity is included for each Christian hero in this activity guide. At the end of each missionary adventure that the children experience, the children will have keepsakes to put in their shoeboxes of memories. If you prefer, you may choose a different container in which the children can store their keepsakes.

Materials

❖ The house pattern (see following page) copied onto white construction paper (one for each child)
❖ Red construction paper
❖ Scissors
❖ Crayons or colored pencils
❖ Glue

Steps to Follow

1. Take the house pattern and cut on the solid lines where indicated. Then fold the pattern on the dotted lines where indicated.

2. Use crayons or colored pencils to draw two windows on the house. Then draw a scene in each window (e.g., a family eating, children playing, or a mother and father smiling with children).

3. Add other details to the house using crayons, glue, and scraps of construction paper.

4. Add shutters and a chimney cut from red construction paper.

5. Now have the children take the promise or comfort notes they wrote or drew (see Character Activity on previous page) and glue it on the inside of their house.

6. When the houses are completed, have the children put them in their shoeboxes to remember how Amy built a loving home for the orphans. (If the children have written their cards for someone special, let them take the cards home, but try to make sure they make an extra promise or comfort note to put in their shoeboxes.)

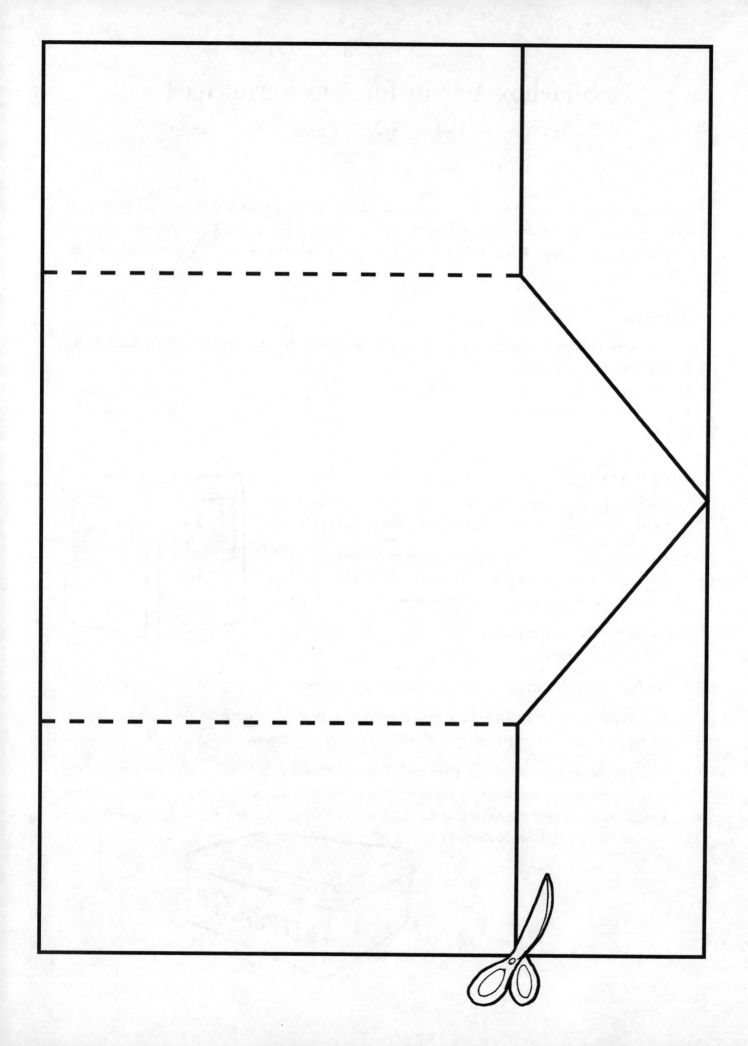

Fascinating Facts about India

❖ Indians do not shake hands like we do. They instead fold their palms together and say the word *namaste* ("I bow my head to you"). When meeting people older than they are, Indians will often touch the elder's feet out of respect. Also, white hair is a symbol of age and wisdom.

❖ In India, boys who practice the Sikh religion never cut their hair. When they turn five years old, they are given their first turban to wrap up their hair.

❖ In India, if children follow the Hindu religion, their heads are shaved when they are young. Hindus believe it is unhealthy and unlucky to keep hair.

❖ Young Indians are rarely allowed to date, and parents usually decide whom their children will marry. However, most young people can reject their parents' choice. Many young married couples continue to live with the husband's parents even after they have children of their own.

Elephants of India

The elephants of India have smaller ears and weigh less than African elephants. They live in forests, grasslands, and marshes, where they eat grass, leaves, trees, and shrubs. They also like to eat wild mangos.

The female elephants can give birth every four to six years. The babies are carried inside the elephant mothers for almost two years before they are born. These elephants can live as long as sixty to seventy years.

Elephants talk to each other by touch, sound, and scent and can make sounds that humans are unable to hear. When nervous, a young elephant will go to an adult and place the tip of its trunk in the adult's mouth.

In heavily wooded areas, Indian people use elephants to carry heavy logs and transport tourists because elephants can walk in areas where vehicles are unable to travel.

Color the elephants of India on the following page.

Elephants of India

Map: Amy Carmichael

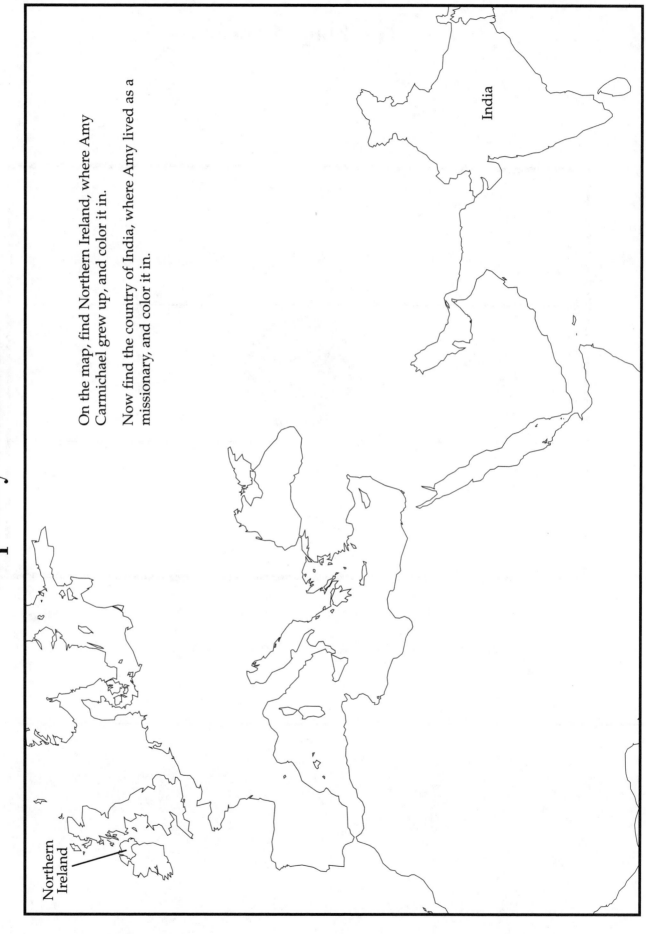

On the map, find Northern Ireland, where Amy Carmichael grew up, and color it in.

Now find the country of India, where Amy lived as a missionary, and color it in.

India

Northern Ireland

The Flag of India

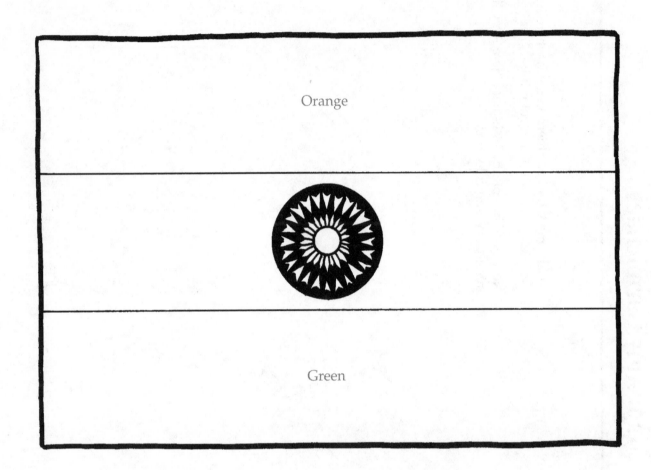

Above is the flag of India. Color the flag orange and green where indicated. Leave the middle section white.

Amy Carmichael Quiz

Color the elephants whose facts are correct.
Draw a big X over the elephants whose facts are incorrect.

Amy wanted to become rich and famous when she grew up.

Amy read the Bible and taught songs to the local children.

Poor people who wore shawls were called shawlies.

Church people were very welcoming to the shawlies.

Many people in India are Hindus.

Hindus thought that what the Christians believed was true.

The young girl, Preena, was locked inside a rich man's house.

When Amy let Preena live with her, she did not have to hide her.

Amy built a nursery, homes, and a hospital for the children in India.

Amy did not keep the promise she made when she was young.

Fun with Rhyme

It's your turn to be a poet. See if you can write down the correct word inside each elephant without looking at your book on Amy Carmichael. Hint: The word rhymes with the last word in the second line.

Word Bank

bed

sight

hide

poor

young

friend

Long silk and colored saris were
    the clothes rich women wore,
but Amy chose to dress in plain
    white cotton like the

She told them about Jesus and
    the blessings He would send
if they would burn their idols and
    let Jesus be their

When evening came, the girl crept out
    and tiptoed through the night.
And as she crossed a bridge, a Christian
    banner came in

One night the girl escaped, but back
    at home her mother said:
"You cannot stay. You must return
    straight to your temple

As Amy's family grew in size
    there wasn't room inside
the little house for all of them
    to live, and sleep, and

And Amy loved her children, she
    loved each and every one,
just as she once had promised when
    she was so very

Amy Carmichael Crossword Puzzle

Word Bank

Ireland

Carmichael

saris

temple

India

Hindus

Jesus

shawlies

need

idol

Across

3. Amy _ _ _ _ _ _ _ _ _.
5. Amy told the Indians about what friend of hers?
8. The country Amy sailed to.
9. A false god.
10. The people of a religion that worships idols.

Down

1. Poor women who could not afford hats.
2. God wants us to help those who are in _ _ _ _.
4. The country Amy came from in Europe.
6. A building dedicated to worship.
7. The name of the clothing that Indian women wear.

Corrie ten Boom: Shining in the Darkness

Corrie ten Boom Song

Corrie was so very brave that during World War Two, she had a secret hiding place where she hid many Jews.

A closet that was near her bedroom hid the secret space. A wall slid back, a secret door led to the hiding place.

The hiding place, the hiding place, Corrie kept a hiding place. With God she chose to do what's right and hid the Jews from sight.

The hiding place, the hiding place, Corrie kept a hiding place, a place where Jews could safely stay till liberation day.

The Good Character Quality
of Corrie ten Boom

Definition of Courageous: Able to stand up for something even when you are afraid.

Bible Verse: "Be strong and courageous" (Joshua 1:6).

Materials

❖ Copy of the crown, strip, and emerald jewel labeled "courage" on page 30 for each child (use heavy white paper or card stock; if you do not wish to have the children color their crowns, use heavy yellow paper or yellow card stock)
❖ Scissors
❖ Crayons or colored pencils
❖ Stapler
❖ Tape or glue

Steps to Follow

1. Introduce the character quality of courage, which describes Corrie, and discuss its meaning with the children. Read aloud the Bible verse above.

2. Have the children color and cut out the emerald labeled "courage." (Because it is an emerald, you may want to suggest they color it green.)

3. Have the children color and cut out the crown and strip. Read aloud the following Bible verse: "Be faithful … and I will give you the crown of life" (Rev. 2:10).

4. Have the children tape or glue the emerald to the crown. Then have them staple the strip to the crown and put it around their heads. The crowns will serve as their "thinking caps" about courage.

5. Ask the children, "How did Corrie demonstrate courage in her life through her words and actions?"
   ❖ She risked serious punishment or even her life by hiding the Jews.

❖ She risked serious punishment or even her life by hiding her Bible and then reading it aloud in the prison camp.

6. Ask the children if they know someone—a parent, neighbor, or friend—who demonstrates courage in their lives. Have them tell the class about this person.

7. Have the children sing the character song "We'll Be Brave and Strong" on page 31. (This song is sung to the tune of "Do Your Ears Hang Low?" If you have the CD for Corrie ten Boom, you can have the children follow or sing along with this song. At the end of the CD, there is a solo piano accompaniment, which the children can sing along with as well.)

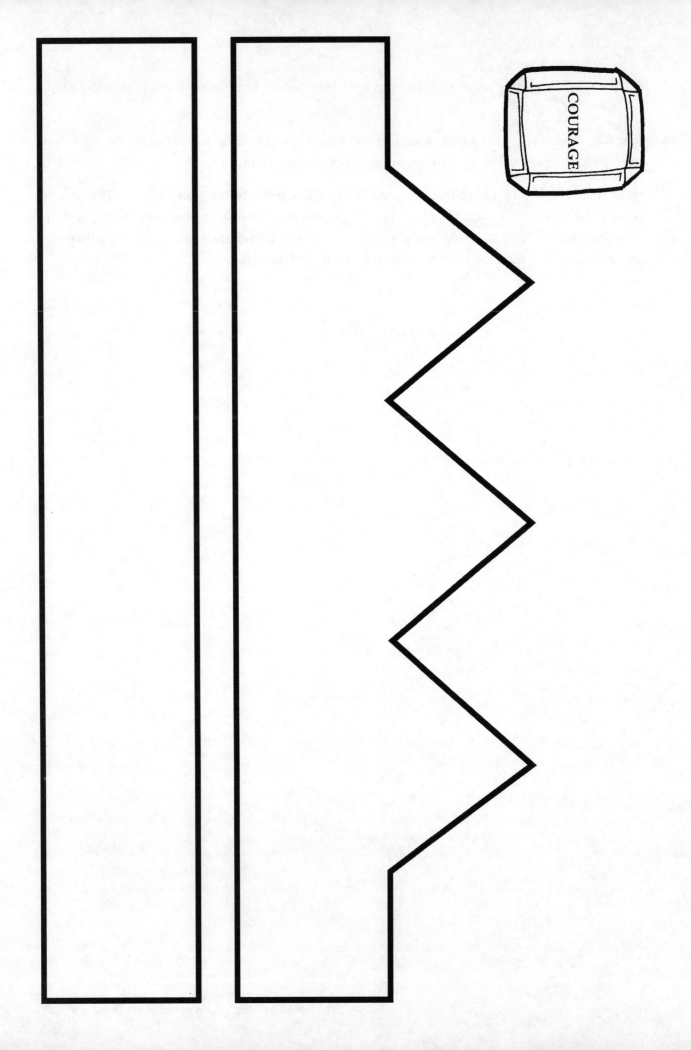

COURAGE

Corrie ten Boom Character Song

We'll Be Brave and Strong

Character Activity for Corrie ten Boom
An Imaginary Journey Inside the Prison Camp

Steps to Follow

1. Tell the children, "We're in Germany during World War Two, and we're all prisoners headed to the camp where Corrie was imprisoned. Let's walk around and show how we feel as prisoners. What do our faces look like? How will we walk? Are we hungry, sad, afraid? Let's show some of these emotions as we go."

2. "The only thing we have with us, hidden inside our clothes, is our Bible." (This can be an imaginary Bible, a real Bible, or one made from the Shoebox Activity following this section.) "Our Bible is the one thing that will give us the strength and courage to face whatever lies ahead."

3. "I see the camp in the distance and a prison guard. We must be able to get our Bibles past the guard's inspection." (Either have one or two of the children act as guards, standing opposite one another, or just pretend there is a guard.) "Let's pray, 'God, send your angels here. Please give us your protection.'"

4. "The guard looks quite gruff and is carefully searching the woman ahead of us. Okay, it's our turn now. Let's walk single file past him, doing our best to look as calm as possible." (Let the children walk by the guard(s) while he searches them but fails to find the Bibles.)

5. "The guard(s) didn't find our Bibles! We made it!"

6. "Now we need to go inside our barracks. Oh, there are fleas everywhere, jumping on us." (Lightly swat at your face and body and have the children imitate you.)

7. "Let's try to ignore the fleas and sit on the floor."

8. "I hear a guard marching outside." (Have the guard stand in one place and lightly stomp his or her feet, or have it be imaginary.)

9. "I think the guard's footsteps are getting quieter and going away. So let's read from our Bible from Psalm 18, verse 2: 'The Lord is my rock, my fortress and my deliverer; my God is my rock, in whom I take refuge.'"

10. "I don't hear the guard anymore. I think he's left and won't come in because of all the fleas in here." Ask the children, "Does anyone have a Bible verse that they would like to read?" (The children may read from a real Bible or one from the Shoebox Activity, or they may know a Bible verse by heart.)

11. "I'm grateful that the fleas are keeping the guards away from our barracks so that we can read the Bible out loud without any fear."

12. "It's time to go to sleep, so let's lie down on the floor. As we do, I'm going to read one last Bible verse from Psalm 4:8: 'I will lie down and sleep in peace, for you alone, O Lord, make me dwell in safety.'"

Note: You may wish to repeat this exercise and have the children change roles.

Shoebox Activity for Corrie ten Boom
Making a Bible

Materials

❖ White paper or colored construction paper (one sheet for each child)

❖ Colored pencils

❖ Glue or rubber cement (only needed if the children can't write)

❖ The following Bible verses written out on pieces of paper:

"Fear not, for I have redeemed you; I have summoned you by name; you are mine." (Is. 43:1)

"Even though I walk through the valley of the shadow of death, I will fear no evil, for you are with me." (Ps. 23: 4)

"The Lord is my light and my salvation—whom shall I fear?" (Ps. 27:1)

"The Lord is my rock, my fortress and my deliverer; my God is my rock, in whom I take refuge." (Ps. 18:2)

"As a mother comforts her child, so will I comfort you." (Is. 66:13)

"I will lie down and sleep in peace, for you alone, O Lord, make me dwell in safety." (Ps. 4:8)

"I have set the Lord always before me. Because he is at my right hand, I will not be shaken." (Ps. 16:8)

❖ Basket to put Bible verses in

Steps to Follow

1. Ask the children, "What was it that Corrie hid from the Germans?" After they have answered, ask them, "Why do you think the Bible was so important to Corrie that she would risk her life to keep it?"

2. Have a basket containing Bible verses (listed above) written on small pieces of paper. Have each child take one or two Bible verses from the basket, depending on how many children you have.

3. Have the children read their Bible verses out loud. If they can't read, you can read the verses for them.

4. Have the children each take a sheet of white paper or colored construction paper and fold the paper in half. Then have them fold the paper again to form a small booklet.

5. Have the children write "Bible" on the front of their booklets.

6. Inside their Bibles, have them write down their Bible verse(s). If they cannot write, have them glue on the papers with their Bible verse(s).

7. Have the children put their Bibles into their shoeboxes to remind them of how the Bible was a real comfort and strength to Corrie, especially in the prison camp.

Tulips of Holland

When we think of Holland, we often think of windmills, wooden shoes, Dutch chocolate—and the famous Dutch tulips. The word *tulip* comes from the word *tuliban*, meaning turban. These flowers were grown in Asia and the Mediterranean for centuries before they ever arrived in Holland.

Tulips grow well in Holland because of the cool spring temperatures. In fact, they can grow well in any soil type as long as it has good drainage. Tulip bulbs are planted in the ground three to four inches apart. Once the tulips have bloomed in the spring, the bulbs can stay in the ground throughout the year with just a little fertilizer to keep them healthy through the Dutch winters.

Follow the instructions below to create your own decorative spring tulips that can grow whenever you want them to.

Materials

❖ White cardstock paper (one sheet for each child)
❖ Pencils
❖ Colored pencils or crayons
❖ Scissors
❖ Glue
❖ Tongue depressor or craft stick (one for each child)
❖ Paper cup (one for each child)

Steps to Follow

1. Draw the outline of a tulip (without a stem) on a piece of white card stock, making it smaller in diameter than the cup.

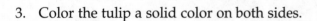

2. Cut out the outline of the tulip.

3. Color the tulip a solid color on both sides.

4. Glue the tulip to the end of a tongue depressor or craft stick.

5. Cut a thin slit in the bottom of the cup (if the children are very young, an adult should do this for them), making it wide enough for the tongue depressor to slide through.

6. Slide the tulip into the cup, pushing the stem (tongue depressor) through the slit in the bottom. Now watch the tulip grow by slowly pushing the tulip stem up through the slit in the cup.

Map: Corrie ten Boom

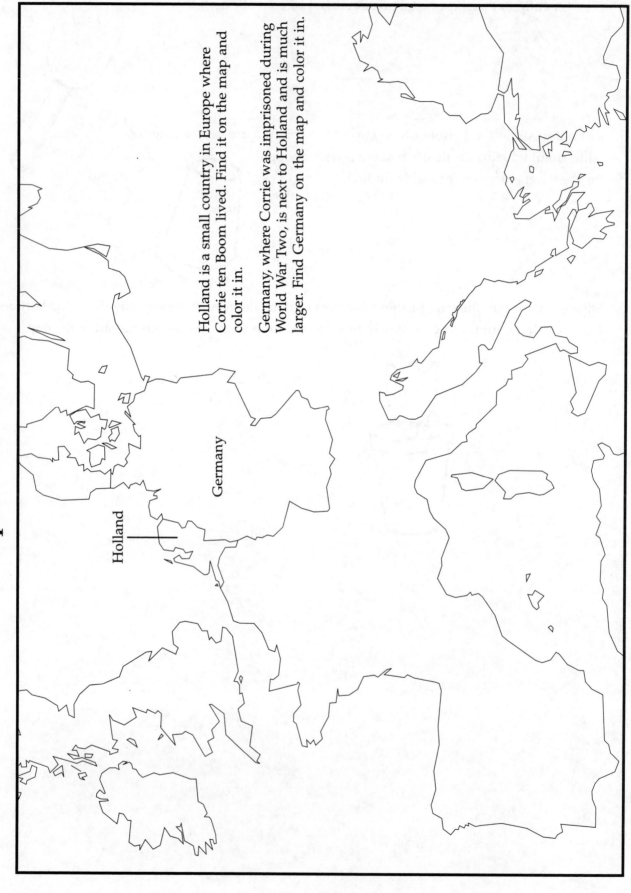

Holland is a small country in Europe where Corrie ten Boom lived. Find it on the map and color it in.

Germany, where Corrie was imprisoned during World War Two, is next to Holland and is much larger. Find Germany on the map and color it in.

Holland

Germany

The Flag of Holland

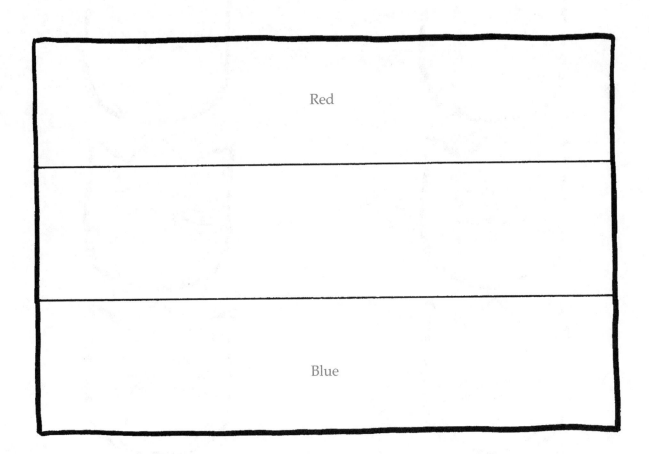

Above is the flag of Holland. Color the flag red and blue where indicated. Leave the middle part white.

Corrie ten Boom Quiz

Color the tulips whose facts are correct.
Draw a big X over the tulips whose facts are incorrect.

Germany invaded Holland during World War Two.

Corrie hid her radio in her bedroom.

The Ten Booms were arrested for hiding the Jews.

Corrie's secret room was called the "Angels' Den."

The Germans were nice to the Ten Booms when they arrested them.

Corrie told the Germans where the Jews were hidden.

The Bible helped give Corrie peace in prison.

Corrie hid her Bible from the Germans, but they found it.

After the war, Corrie forgot all about people without homes or jobs.

The secret word for Jews that the Ten Booms used was "clocks."

Fun with Rhyme

It's your turn to be a poet. See if you can fill in the correct word inside each tulip without looking at you book on Corrie ten Boom. Hint: The word rhymes with the last word in the second line.

Word Bank

near
still
done
room
day
way

A famous architect arrived.
    He set to work and soon
he'd built upstairs, near Corrie's bed,
    a hidden, secret

When Corrie read the Bible in
    her cell, it eased her fear.
It made her feel a sense of peace
    to know that God is

She saw long rows of clapboard buildings
    painted ugly gray.
A wall with sharp barbed wire would
    enclose them night and

But Betsie said to Corrie as
    they stumbled down the hill,
"No pit's so deep that God's great love
    will not be deeper

And on December twenty-eighth
    before the New Year's Day,
as Betsie said, they both were free,
    each one in her own

The years passed by and Corrie died,
    when she was ninety-one.
Her life blessed many people through
    the brave, kind deeds she'd

Corrie ten Boom Crossword Puzzle

Word Bank

Holland

Ravensbruck

Bible

Germany

plight

architect

Jews

fleas

forty-five*

God

*no hyphen in crossword

Across

3. The land of the Dutch.
7. A difficult situation.
8. The name of the prison Corrie was taken to.
10. Who were the people that Corrie hid?

Down

1. World War Two ended in nineteen _ _ _ _ _ - _ _ _ _ .
2. The love of _ _ _ is deeper than the deepest pit.
4. Someone who designs buildings.
5. Home country of the Nazi party.
6. Why wouldn't the guards come into Corrie's barracks?
9. What did Corrie sneak into the prison?

Mary Slessor: Courage in Africa

Mary Slessor Song

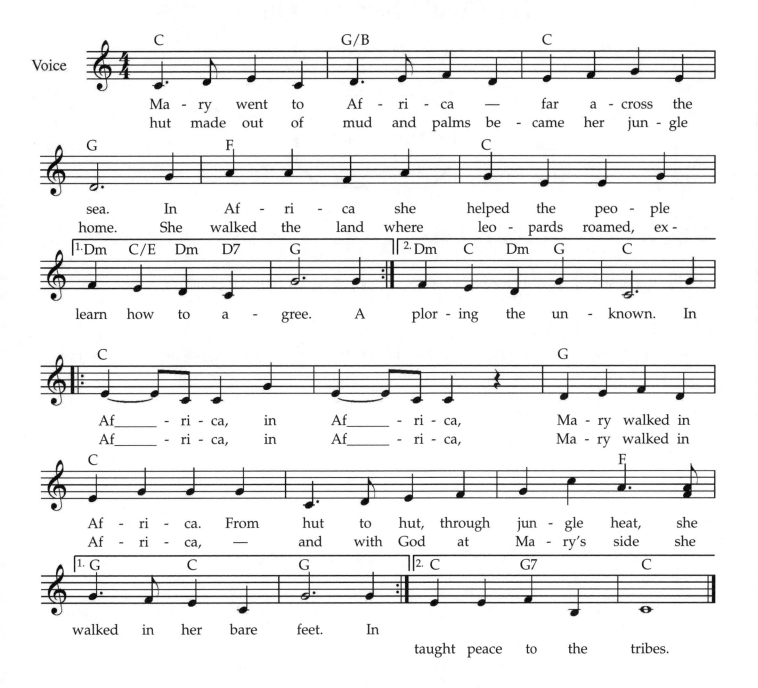

Mary went to Africa, far across the sea. In Africa she helped the people learn how to agree.

A hut made out of mud and palms became her jungle home. She walked the land where leopards roamed, exploring the unknown.

In Africa, in Africa, Mary walked in Africa. From hut to hut, through jungle heat, she walked in her bare feet.

In Africa, in Africa, Mary walked in Africa, and with God at Mary's side she taught peace to the tribes.

The Good Character Quality
of Mary Slessor

Definition of Peacemaker: A defender and protector who tries to bring peace and order.

Bible Verse: "Blessed are the peacemakers, for they will be called sons of God" (Matthew 5:9).

Materials

❖ Copy of the crown, strip, and ruby jewel labeled "peacemaker" on page 48 for each child (use heavy white paper or card stock; if you do not wish to have the children color their crowns, use heavy yellow paper or yellow card stock)
❖ Scissors
❖ Crayons or colored pencils
❖ Stapler
❖ Tape or glue

Steps to Follow

1. Introduce the character quality of peacemaker, which describes Mary, and discuss its meaning with the children. Read aloud the Bible verse above.

2. Have the children color and cut out the ruby labeled "peacemaker." (Because it is a ruby, tell them they may want to color it red.)

3. Have the children color and cut out the crown and strip. Read aloud the following Bible verses: "Do you not know that in a race all the runners run, but only one gets the prize? Run in such a way as to get the prize. Everyone who competes in the games goes into strict training. They do it to get a crown that will not last; but we do it to get a crown that will last forever" (1 Corinthians 9:24–25).

4. Have the children tape or glue the ruby to the crown. Then have them staple the strip to the crown and put it around their heads. This will serve as their "thinking cap" about being peacemakers.

5. Ask the children, "How did Mary show that she was a peacemaker through her words and actions?"

❖ She walked from tribe to tribe to talk of peace with everyone she met.

❖ She taught the chiefs they should not kill and encouraged them to sit and talk with one another.

6. Ask the children if they know someone—a parent, neighbor, or friend—who shows they are a peacemaker. Have them tell the class about this person.

7. Ask the children if they can think of ways they can be peacemakers in their own lives, such as:

❖ Responding without being mean when others treat us unfairly

❖ Making sure our speech is always kind and considerate

❖ Trying to see another's point of view when we disagree

8. Have the children sing the character song "We'll Be Peacemakers" on page 49. (This song is sung to the tune of "Do Your Ears Hang Low?" If you have the CD for Mary Slessor, you can have the children follow or sing along with this song. At the end of the CD, there is a solo piano accompaniment, which the children can sing along with as well.)

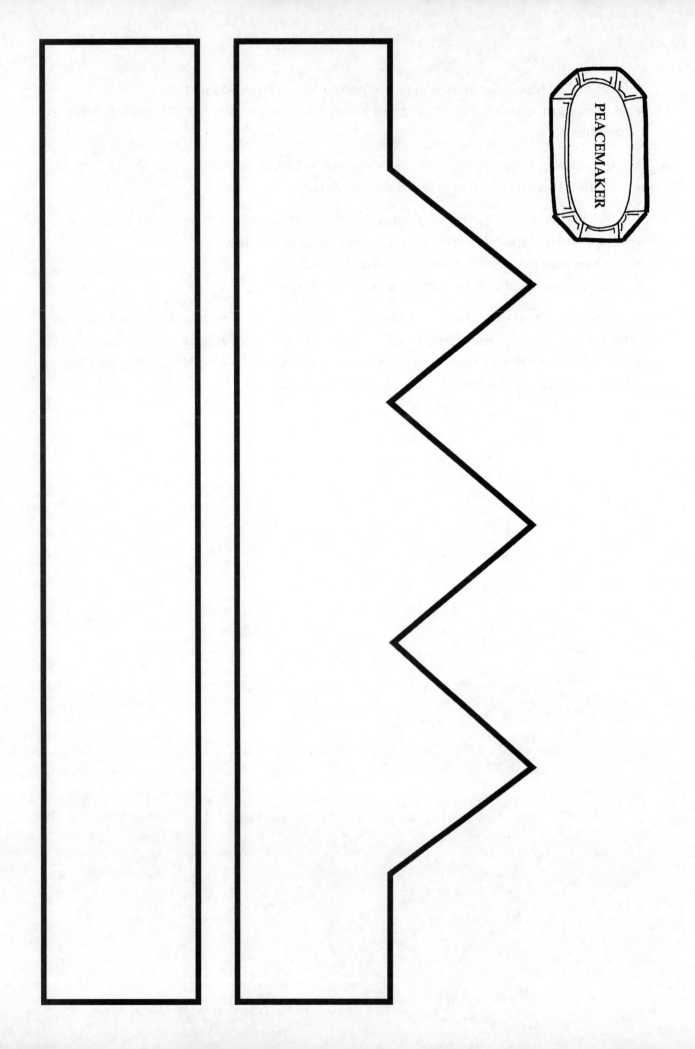

PEACEMAKER

Mary Slessor Character Song

We'll Be Peacemakers

Character Activity for Mary Slessor

Walking from Hut to Hut as a Peacemaker

Mary lived in a mud and palm-thatched hut in Africa. For this activity, to remember how Mary was a peacemaker and served the Africans, we will make our own African hut.

Materials

- ❖ Round cardboard container; a larger container, such as an oatmeal canister, can be cut in half to make two (one for each child)
- ❖ Brown construction paper (one sheet for each child)
- ❖ Raffia or long thin strips of green paper
- ❖ Crayons or colored pencils
- ❖ Glue
- ❖ Scissors
- ❖ Regular tape
- ❖ Double-stick tape

Steps to Follow

1. Have the children cut a piece of brown construction paper to fit around the circumference of the container, and glue or tape (with double-stick tape) it around the outside.

3. Draw an arched door on the paper.

4. Use crayons or colored pencils to decorate the container.

5. Take a piece of brown construction paper and draw a large circle on it, about twice the diameter of the container.

6. Make a cut to the center of the circle (see picture with dotted line).

7. Take the edges and bring them together to form a cone shape until the base of the cone is the same size as the container. Tape the cone closed along the outer edge.

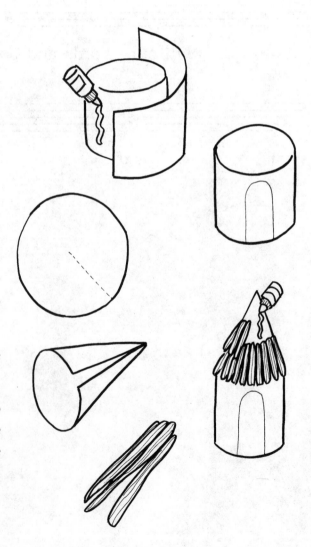

8. Tape the cone to the top of the container. Now you have a hut with a roof.

9. Glue long thin pieces of raffia or green construction paper to the roof.

10. When all the children have finished building their huts, divide the class in half. Tell them that they are now living in African villages like the ones Mary visited. Have one half display their huts on their desks while the other half walks around and ask them questions about their village, such as:

    ❖ Are there any disagreements between you and the other villagers?
    ❖ Is there any fighting between other villagers that I need to know about?
    ❖ What are some ways that you are peacemakers in your village?

Shoebox Activity for Mary Slessor
Finding Jungle Animals

Materials

❖ Copy of the jungle picture on the following page for each child
❖ Crayons or colored pencils

Steps to Follow

1. Pass out a copy of the jungle picture to each child. Explain to them, "Mary showed great courage as she walked through jungle forests to visit different villages. There were many animals along the way—some friendly and some not so friendly."

2. Tell the children to color every animal they can find.

3. After the children have finished coloring their animals, have them put their pictures into their shoeboxes. This will remind them of how Mary bravely walked through jungle forests to serve the African people.

Mary Slessor's African Jungle

African Musical Instrument

Making a Rattle

Here's a musical instrument that Mary Slessor could have used to keep the leopards away while she was walking in the jungle—a rattle.

Materials

- ❖ Cardboard bathroom-tissue tube (one for each child)
- ❖ Paints or crayons
- ❖ Dry rice or dry beans
- ❖ Clear masking tape
- ❖ Colored construction paper
- ❖ Scissors
- ❖ Glue
- ❖ Pencils

Steps to Follow

1. Decorate the paper tube with paint, crayons, and colored construction paper. If the children use paint, make sure it dries before continuing to the next step.

2. Using the end of the tube, trace two circles onto construction paper. Cut out the circles.

3. Close one end of the tube by taping one of the paper circles to it. Make sure the circle is securely taped around the edge.

4. Put a handful of dry rice or dry beans inside the tube.

5. Close the tube by securely taping the second paper circle to the open end of the tube.

6. Now the children can shake their new instruments and hear the rattle sound that is still heard today in some African music.

Map: Mary Slessor

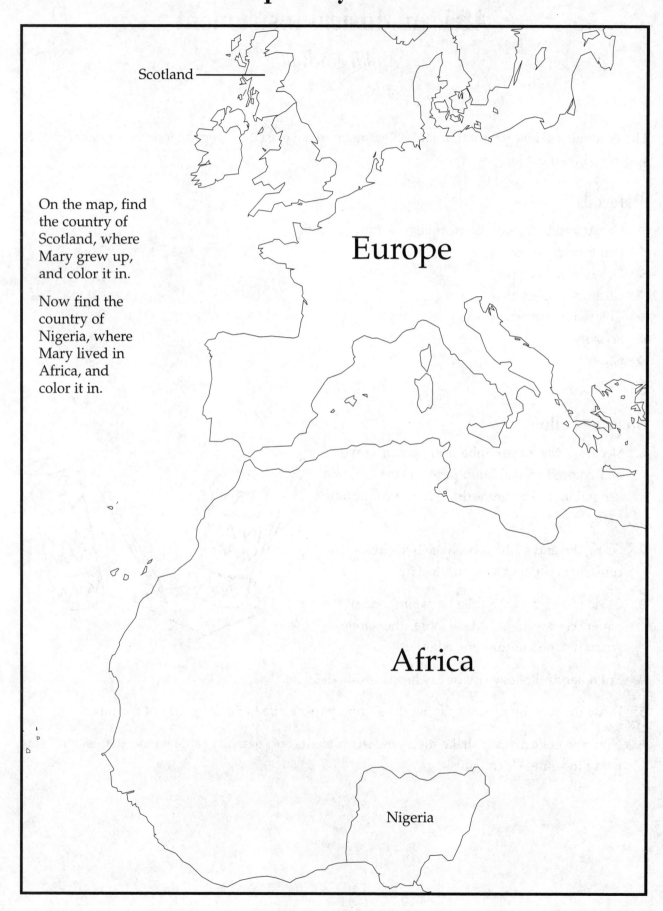

Scotland ———

Europe

On the map, find
the country of
Scotland, where
Mary grew up,
and color it in.

Now find the
country of
Nigeria, where
Mary lived in
Africa, and
color it in.

Africa

Nigeria

The Flag of Nigeria

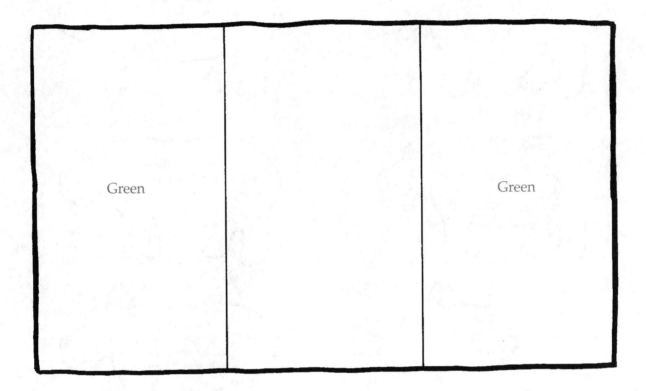

Above is the flag of Nigeria. Color it green where indicated. Leave the middle part white.

Mary Slessor Quiz

Color the hippopotamuses whose facts are correct.
Draw a big X over the hippopotamuses whose facts are incorrect.

Before Mary went to Africa, she was a nurse.

Leopards made it dangerous to walk on the trails in Africa.

Mary was from Ireland.

Mary visited villages where no other outsiders dared to go.

The natives called Mary "White Ma."

The Africans felt that their gods were pleased when they did cruel things.

The Africans gave special honor to twin babies.

British rulers asked Mary to work with the tribes as a translator.

When walking through the forest, Mary avoided kangaroos and chimpanzees.

Mary worked as a teacher, nurse, peace-maker, and judge among the African people.

Fun with Rhyme

It's your turn to be a poet. See if you can fill in the correct word inside each hippopotamus without looking at your book on Mary Slessor. Hint: The word rhymes with the last word in the second line.

Word Bank

fed
do
loud
door
ground
ill

When Mary ran inside and saw
    a small, determined crowd,
she grabbed the twins away from them
    and wildly yelled out

Soon children who were orphaned or
    whose parents were too poor
were brought to Mary's tiny hut
    and left at her front

One day an urgent message came
    requesting Mary's skill
to help out at a village where
    the chief was gravely

She followed through the forest as
    a guide led on ahead,
avoiding snakes and crocodiles
    looking to be

Then with a cry of great disgust
    the warrior turned around;
he left, and Mary hastened toward
    the woman on the

As Mary did, God wants us all
    to show great courage too,
especially when to do what's right
    is difficult to

Mary Slessor Crossword Puzzle

Word Bank

chief

Scotland

judge

alien

canoe

leopard

courage

hut

Africa

crocodile

Across

1. Unfamiliar.
5. A large reptile with thick armor-like skin.
6. Mary's new jungle home.
8. A light, slender boat with pointed ends.
9. A position Mary took to bring peace to the tribes.

Down

1. The continent Mary sailed to.
2. Part of Great Britain and Mary's homeland.
3. Brave Mary showed great _ _ _ _ _ _ _.
4. A large spotted cat.
7. The person in charge of a tribe.

William Carey: Bearer of Good News

William Carey Song

William went to India, and when he tried to preach, the Hindus were polite but did not understand his speech.

And so he learned their language well and gave them something new: a Bible in their language so that they could read it too.

The Bible, the Bible, the good news of the Bible. God's great book was passed by hand throughout that spacious land.

The Bible, the Bible, the good news of the Bible. In India they know it's true that Jesus loves them too.

The Good Character Quality
of William Carey

Definition of Diligence: Working steadily and tirelessly to complete a task.

Bible Verse: "Lazy hands make a man poor, but diligent hands bring wealth" (Proverbs 10:4).

Materials

❖ Copy of the crown, strip, and opal jewel labeled "diligence" on page 64 for each child (use heavy white paper or card stock; if you do not wish to have the children color their crowns, use heavy yellow paper or yellow card stock)

❖ Scissors

❖ Crayons or colored pencils

❖ Stapler

❖ Tape or glue

Steps to Follow

1. Introduce the character quality of diligence, which describes William, and discuss its meaning with the children. Read aloud the Bible verse above.

2. Have the children color and cut out the opal labeled "diligence." (Because it is an opal, tell them they may want to color it milky white or pastel.)

3. Have the children color and cut out the crown and strip. Read aloud the following scripture verse: "And when the Chief Shepherd appears, you will receive the crown of glory that will never fade away" (1 Peter 5:4).

4. Have the children tape or glue the opal to the crown. Then have them staple the strip to the crown and put it around their heads. This will serve as their "thinking cap" about diligence.

5. Ask the children, "How did William show diligence in his life through his words and actions?"
   ❖ He learned three languages before he went to India.
   ❖ Even though not a single Hindu became a Christian when he preached for the first four years, William did not give up.

- He learned two languages when he lived in India and then translated the Bible.
- When his print shop burned down and he lost much of his work, he started all over again and continued the work was completed.

6. Ask the children to think of at least three ways in which they could be more diligent, such as:
   - Doing their chores right away
   - Keeping their rooms clean
   - Consistently brushing their teeth
   - Putting their dirty clothes in the hamper right away
   - Finishing their homework on time without constant reminding

7. Have the children sing the character song "We'll Show Diligence" on page 65. (This song is sung to the tune of "Do Your Ears Hang Low?" If you have the CD for William Carey, you can have the children follow or sing along with this song. At the end of the CD, there is a solo piano accompaniment, which the children can sing along with as well.)

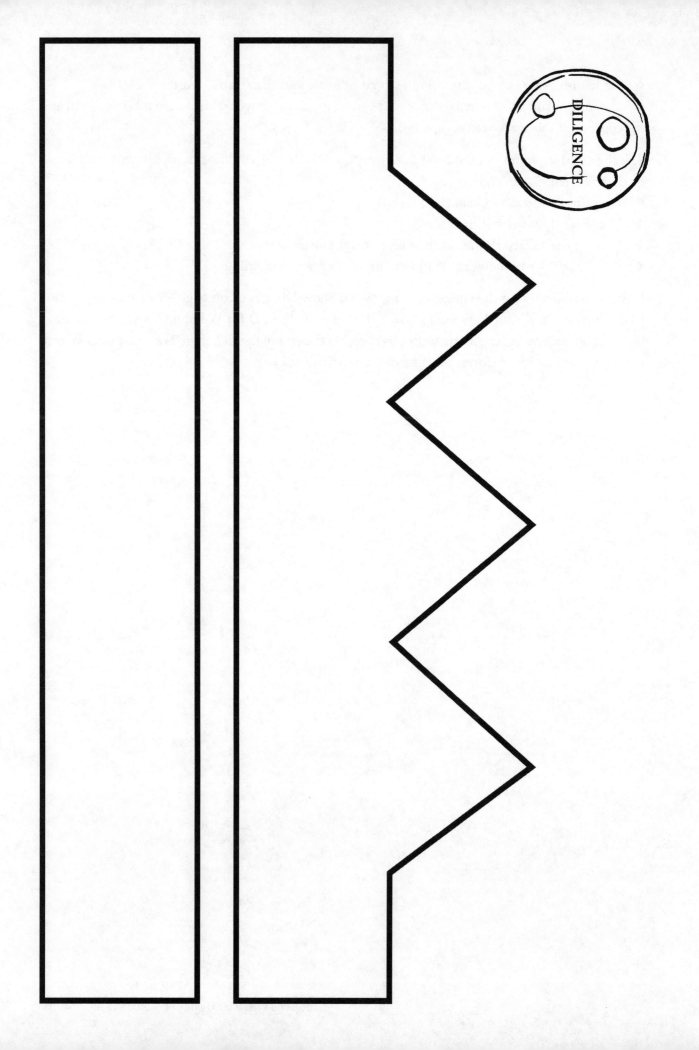

DILIGENCE

William Carey Character Song

We'll Show Diligence

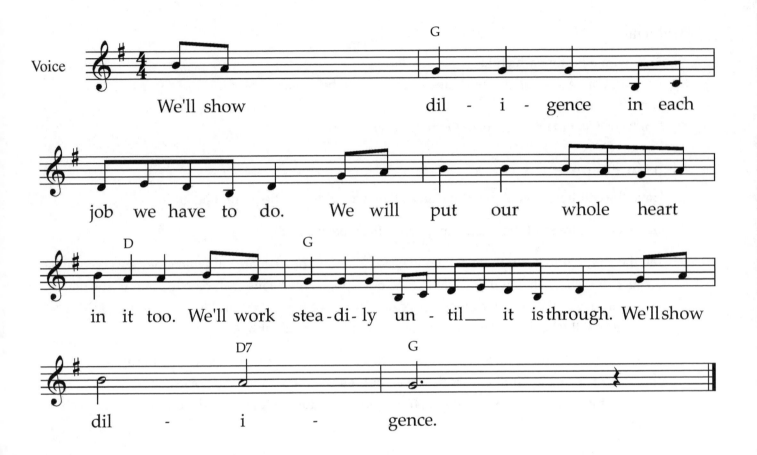

Character Activity for William Carey

Applying Diligence to our Lives

Materials

- ❖ A jar with a lid for each child
- ❖ Any kind of beans—jellybeans, kidney beans, pinto beans, etc.
- ❖ Pens or pencils
- ❖ Small sheets of plain white paper (one for each child)

Steps to Follow

1. Have the children write down three areas they would like to be more diligent in.

2. Have the children put their list, along with fifteen beans, in their jars.

3. Tell the children they are to take out one bean each day for each area in which they successfully practice diligence. They will be able to take out up to three beans each day. Explain to the children that they will do this for the next five days (or have them go from Monday through Friday) and that it will take diligence to follow up on this assignment at home.

4. At the end of five days, have them count and see how few beans they have left in their jar. The object is for the children to empty their jars, but tell them they must be honest about taking out a bean at the end of the day only when they have been diligent in one of the areas listed on their cards.

Shoebox Activity for William Carey

Translating the Bible

Supplies

- A copy of the coded message for each child (see next page)
- Pens or pencils
- Optional: three small prizes for first, second, and third place

Steps to Follow

1. Give each child a copy of the coded message (on the following page) and a pen or pencil to write with.

2. Read the directions (and answer any questions) and have the children translate the message. The message they will be transcribing is from Psalm 23:1 and Mark 10:16: "The Lord is my Shepherd. He took the children in his arms, put his hands on them and blessed them."

3. Have the children fold their translated messages in half or quarters to put in their shoeboxes to remind them of the important work William did in translating the Bible into other languages.

Optional: Tell the children they are going to be in a contest to see who can transcribe the coded message the fastest and to raise their hand as soon as they are finished.

Coded Message

F T Q   X A D P   U E   Y K   E T Q B T Q D P

_ _ _   _ _ _ _   _ _   _ _   _ _ _ _ _ _ _ .

T Q   F A A W   F T Q   O T U X P D Q Z   U Z   T U E

_ _   _ _ _ _   _ _ _   _ _ _ _ _ _ _   _ _   _ _ _

M D Y E   B G F   T U E   T M Z P E   A Z   F T Q Y   M Z P

_ _ _ _ ,   _ _ _   _ _ _   _ _ _ _ _   _ _   _ _ _ _   _ _ _

N X Q E E Q P   F T Q Y

_ _ _ _ _ _ _   _ _ _ _ .

Now it's your turn to be a translator like William Carey. Figure out the message above by finding each alphabet letter in the list below on the left side of the equals sign. Then look at the letter on the right and write it in the appropriate blank space above.

For example, the first letter above is F. In the chart below, F equals (or becomes) a T. Write T in the blank under F.

A = O	J = X	S = G
B = P	K = Y	T = H
C = Q	L = Z	U = I
D = R	M = A	V = J
E = S	N = B	W = K
F = T	O = C	X = L
G = U	P = D	Y = M
H = V	Q = E	Z = N
I = W	R = F	

English Scrimshaw

During the 1800s, while William Carey was living in India, the art of scrimshaw was developed in his home country of England by British-American whalers. The whalers carved objects from pieces of whalebone. By using a jackknife or some other sharp instrument, they etched designs into the piece. Then they smoothed and polished the whalebone with a file and rubbed the design with a coloring to make it stand out. The whalers often carved sailing ships, whales, birds, and other scenes of water or nature.

Materials

❖ White pvc connector pipe, 2 inches long, 3/4 inch in diameter (one for each child)
❖ Permanent markers
❖ Leather cord or shoestring (about one foot for each child)

Steps to Follow

1. Use markers to draw a picture or design on the pvc connector (this can be as simple as stars at night, a sun, or a moon).

2. Pull the cord through the pipe and tie the ends. The new scrimshaw can become a necklace or a key chain decoration.

Map: William Carey

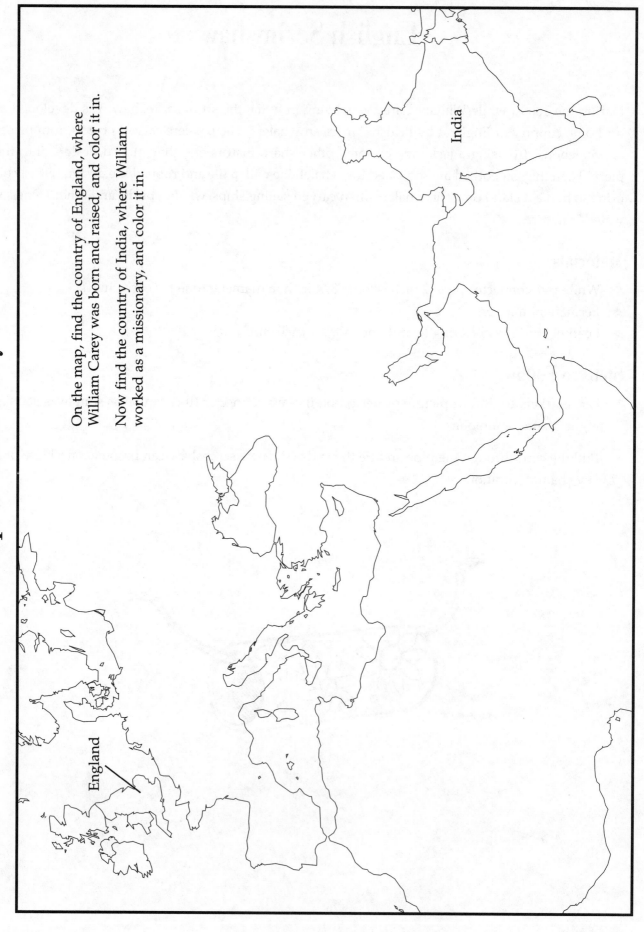

On the map, find the country of England, where William Carey was born and raised, and color it in.

Now find the country of India, where William worked as a missionary, and color it in.

England

India

The Flag of England

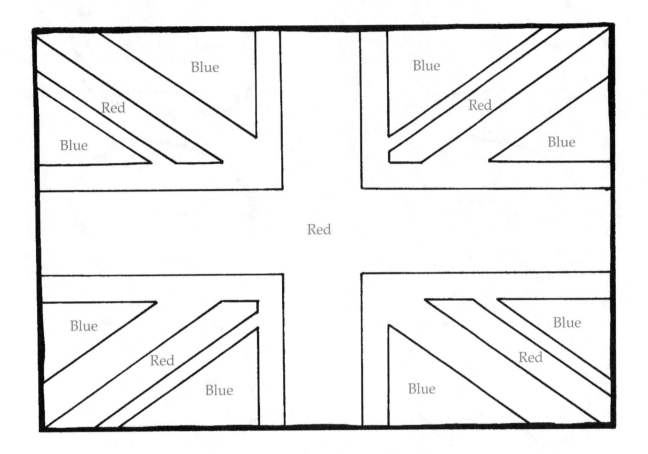

Above is the flag of England. Color the flag red and blue where indicated.

William Carey Quiz

Color only the turbans whose facts are correct.
Draw a big X over the turbans whose facts are incorrect.

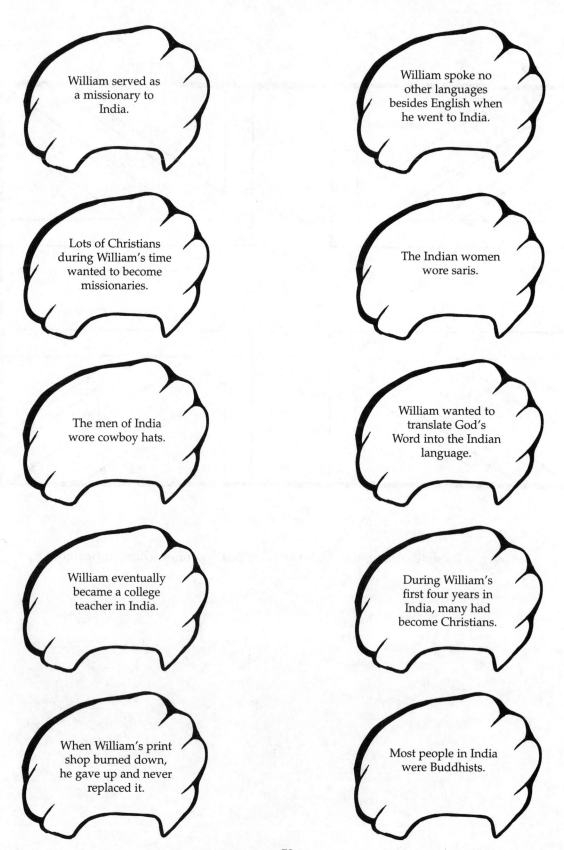

William served as a missionary to India.

William spoke no other languages besides English when he went to India.

Lots of Christians during William's time wanted to become missionaries.

The Indian women wore saris.

The men of India wore cowboy hats.

William wanted to translate God's Word into the Indian language.

William eventually became a college teacher in India.

During William's first four years in India, many had become Christians.

When William's print shop burned down, he gave up and never replaced it.

Most people in India were Buddhists.

Fun with Rhyme

It's your turn to be a poet. See if you can fill in the correct word inside each turban without looking at your book on William Carey. Hint: The word rhymes with the last word in the second line.

Word Bank

about
fear
own
face
read
do

Now William kept on teaching and
    one day nearby his place,
he asked a Hindu, "What's that white
    mark painted on your

"It is a sign of worship and
    it honors our gods too.
Our holy book, the *shastras*, tells
    us it's what we should

As William listened with respect
    he took his Bible out.
"The God of love is what this Christian
    shastras tells

The Hindu listened in return,
    was courteous, sincere,
but wasn't ready to give up
    his gods because of

Translations of the Bible had
    been printed and then spread
throughout the land of India
    and are, today, well

Still many speak in languages
    that are to us unknown
without a written alphabet
    or language of their

William Carey Crossword Puzzle

Word Bank

Bengali

baskets

translate

turban

Sanskrit

teacher

Kali

devout

England

shastras

Across

2. William's job at a college in India.
4. Something Indian women balanced on their heads.
7. The name of William's homeland.
9. The name of a god that the Hindus were afraid of.
10. A long scarf wound directly around the head.

Down

1. To express in another language.
3. A language that wealthy Indians understood.
5. An Indian language William first learned.
6. The name of the Hindu holy book.
8. Deeply religious.

Can You Name the Hero?

See if you can write the correct name of each hero in the space provided from the clues in each stanza.

Can you name the hero who translated the Word
    in the land of India where Hindus had not heard?
Can you name this man who gave them something new—
    a Bible in their language so that they could read it too?

His name was _____. He gave them the Good News.

Can you name the hero who helped hide many Jews,
    who kept a secret hiding place during World War Two?
Can you name this woman who chose to do what's right,
    who as a Christian honored God and hid the Jews from sight?

Her name was _____. She kept a hiding place.

Can you name the hero who taught peace to the tribes
    in the land of Africa with our God at her side?
Can you name this redhead who bravely persevered
    as a teacher, nurse, and judge—she did not live in fear?

Her name was _____. She taught peace to the tribes.

Can you name the hero who rescued many girls
    in the land of India from their unhappy world?
Can you name this Irish lass who always loved to give
    her time, herself to children who had no good place to live?

Her name was _____. She rescued Indian girls.

Note: This exercise can also be sung by following along on the companion CD for books 5–8. When the chorus is repeated the second time, the answers are included.

Answers to "Can You Name the Hero?"

1. William Carey

2. Corrie ten Boom

3. Mary Slessor

4. Amy Carmichael

Answers to Questions

Answers to Amy Carmichael

Amy Carmichael Quiz: Correct Facts

❖ Amy read the Bible and taught songs to the local children.
❖ Poor people who wore shawls were called shawlies.
❖ Many people in India are Hindus.
❖ Amy built a nursery, homes, and hospital for the children in India.

Fun with Rhyme

1. poor
2. friend
3. sight
4. bed
5. hide
6. young

Crossword

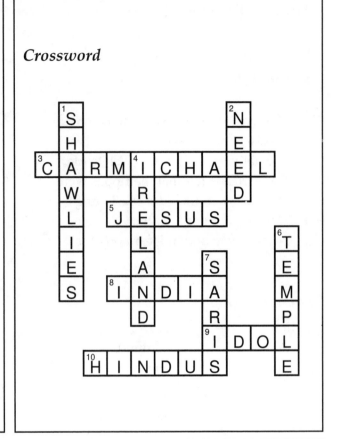

Answers to Corrie ten Boom

Corrie ten Boom Quiz: Correct Facts

❖ Germany invaded Holland during World War Two.
❖ The Ten Booms were arrested for hiding the Jews.
❖ Corrie's secret room was called the "Angels' Den."
❖ The Bible helped give Corrie peace in prison.
❖ The secret word for Jews that the Ten Booms used was "clocks."

Fun with Rhyme

1. room
2. near
3. day
4. still
5. way
6. done

Crossword

Answers to Mary Slessor

Mary Slessor Quiz: Correct Facts

- ❖ Leopards made it dangerous to walk on the trails in Africa.
- ❖ Mary visited villages where no other outsiders dared to go.
- ❖ The natives called Mary "White Ma."
- ❖ The Africans felt that their gods were pleased when they did cruel things.
- ❖ Mary worked as a teacher, nurse, peacemaker, and judge among the African people.

Fun with Rhyme

1. loud
2. door
3. ill
4. fed
5. ground
6. do

Crossword

Answers to William Carey

William Carey Quiz: Correct Facts

- ❖ William served as a missionary to India.
- ❖ The Indian women wore saris.
- ❖ William wanted to translate God's Word into the Indian language.
- ❖ William eventually became a college teacher in India.

Fun with Rhyme

1. face
2. do
3. about
4. fear
5. read
6. own

Crossword

I Will Follow

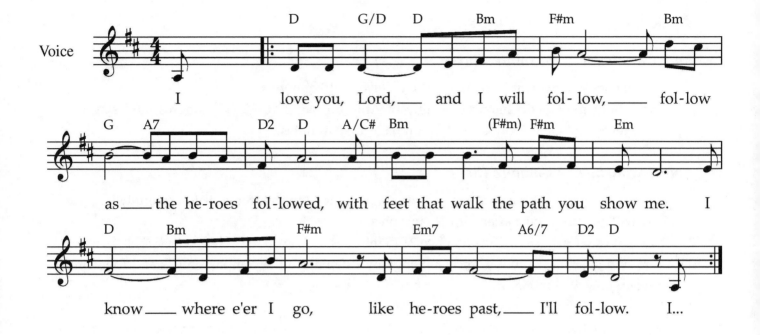

I love you, Lord,____ and I will fol-low,____ fol-low
as ____ the he-roes fol-lowed, with feet that walk the path you show me. I
know ____ where e'er I go, like he-roes past,____ I'll fol-low. I...

2. I love You, Lord, and I will follow,
   follow as the heroes followed,
   with hands that help in ways You guide me.
   I know where e'er I go,
   like heroes past, I'll follow.

3. I love You, Lord, and I will follow,
   follow as the heroes followed,
   with ears that hear the truth You tell me.
   I know where e'er I go,
   like heroes past, I'll follow.

4. I love You, Lord, and I will follow,
   follow as the heroes followed,
   with eyes that see the needs around me.
   I know where e'er I go,
   like heroes past, I'll follow.

Syllabus

Week 1

Amy Carmichael: 30-minute Class

1. Read the book *Amy Carmichael: Rescuing the Children* (10 minutes).
2. Learn about the Good Character Quality of Amy on pages 10–12 (15 minutes) and sing the Character Song "We'll Show Kindness" on page 13 (5 minutes).

Amy Carmichael: 45-minute Class

1. Read the book *Amy Carmichael: Rescuing the Children*. Tell the children to listen carefully because there will be a short quiz afterward (10 minutes).
2. Take the Amy Carmichael Quiz on page 21 (5 minutes).
3. Learn and sing the "Amy Carmichael Song" by listening to the companion CD and following along on page 9 (5 minutes).
4. Do Fun with Rhyme on page 22 (5 minutes).
5. Learn about the Good Character Quality of Amy on pages 10–12 (15 minutes) and sing the Character Song "We'll Show Kindness" on page 13 (5 minutes).

Week 2

Amy Carmichael: 30-minute Class

1. Do the Character Activity on page 14 (15 minutes).
2. Do the Shoebox Activity on pages 15 and 16 (15 minutes).

Amy Carmichael: 45-minute Class

1. Review the "Amy Carmichael Song" on page 9 (5 minutes).
2. Review the Character Song "We'll Show Kindness" on page 13 (5 minutes).
3. Do the Character Activity on page 14 (15 minutes).
4. Do the Shoebox Activity on pages 15 and 16 (15 minutes).
5. Learn and sing the Prayer Song "I Will Follow" by listening to the companion CD and following along on page 79 (5 minutes).

Week 3

Corrie ten Boom: 30-minute Class

1. Read the book *Corrie ten Boom: Shining in the Darkness*. Tell them to listen carefully because there will be a short quiz afterward (10 minutes).

2. Take the Corrie ten Boom Quiz on page 40 (5 minutes).

3. Enact the Character Activity on pages 32 and 33 (10 minutes).

4. Learn and sing the "Corrie ten Boom Song" by listening to the companion CD and following along on page 27 (5 minutes).

Corrie ten Boom: 45-minute Class

1. Read the book *Corrie ten Boom: Shining in the Darkness*. Tell the children to listen carefully because there will be a short quiz afterward (10 minutes).

2. Take the Corrie ten Boom Quiz on page 40 (5 minutes).

3. Learn and sing the "Corrie ten Boom Song" by listening to the companion CD and following along on page 27 (5 minutes).

4. Color the map on page 38 (5 minutes).

5. Enact the Character Activity on pages 32 and 33 (10 minutes).

6. Learn and sing the Character Song "We'll Be Brave and Strong" on page 31 (5 minutes).

7. Review the Prayer Song "I Will Follow" on page 79 (5 minutes).

Week 4

Corrie ten Boom: 30-minute Class

1. Learn about the Good Character Quality of Corrie on pages 28–30 (10 minutes) and sing the Character Song "We'll Be Brave and Strong" on page 31 (5 minutes).

2. Do the Shoebox Activity for Corrie on pages 34 and 35 (15 minutes).

Corrie ten Boom: 45-minute Class

1. Review the "Corrie ten Boom Song" on page 27 (5 minutes).

2. Learn about the Good Character Quality of Corrie on pages 28–30 (10 minutes) and review the Character Song "We'll Be Brave and Strong" on page 31 (5 minutes).

3. Do the Shoebox Activity for Corrie on pages 34 and 35 (15 minutes).

4. Color the flag of Holland on page 39 (5 minutes).
   Optional: While the children are coloring, play the "Corrie ten Boom Song," "We'll Be Brave and Strong," and "I Will Follow" from the companion CD for them to listen to.

5. Review the Prayer Song "I Will Follow" by listening to the companion CD and following along on page 79 (5 minutes).

Week 5

Mary Slessor: 30-minute Class

1. Read the book *Mary Slessor: Courage in Africa* (10 minutes).

2. Learn and sing the "Mary Slessor Song" by listening to the companion CD and following along on page 45 (5 minutes).

3. Learn about the Good Character Quality of Mary on pages 46–48 (10 minutes) and sing the Character Song "We'll Be Peacemakers" on page 49 (5 minutes).

Mary Slessor: 45-minute Class

1. Read the book *Mary Slessor: Courage in Africa*. Tell the children to listen carefully because there will be a short quiz afterward (10 minutes).
2. Take the Mary Slessor Quiz on page 56 (5 minutes).
3. Learn and sing the "Mary Slessor Song" by listening to the companion CD and following along on page 45 (5 minutes).
4. Do Fun with Rhyme on page 57 (5 minutes).
5. Work the Crossword Puzzle on page 58 (10 minutes).
   Please note: For very young children, sing "We'll Be Peacemakers" on page 49 and "I Will Follow" on page 79 instead of working the crossword puzzle.
6. Do the Shoebox Activity on pages 51 and 52 (10 minutes).

Week 6

Mary Slessor: 30-minute Class

1. Do the Character Activity for Mary on pages 50 and 51 (30 minutes).

Mary Slessor: 45-minute Class

1. Learn about the Good Character Quality of Mary on pages 46–48 (10 minutes) and sing the Character Song "We'll Be Peacemakers" on page 49 (5 minutes).
2. Do the Character Activity on pages 50 and 51 (30 minutes).

Week 7

William Carey: 30-minute Class

1. Read the book *William Carey: Bearer of Good News*. Tell the children to listen carefully because there will be a short quiz afterward (10 minutes).
2. Take the William Carey Quiz on page 72 (5 minutes).
3. Learn and sing the "William Carey Song" by listening to the companion CD and following along on page 61 (5 minutes).
4. Do the Shoebox Activity on pages 67 and 68 (10 minutes).

William Carey: 45-minute Class

1. Read the book *William Carey: Bearer of Good News*. Tell the children to listen carefully because there will be a short quiz afterward (10 minutes).

2. Take the William Carey Quiz on page 72 (5 minutes).
3. Learn and sing the "William Carey Song" by listening to the companion CD and following along on page 61 (5 minutes).
4. Learn about the Good Character Quality of William on pages 62–64 (10 minutes) and sing the Character Song "We'll Show Diligence" on page 65 (5 minutes).
5. Do the Character Activity for William on page 66 (10 minutes).

Week 8

William Carey: 30-minute Class

1. Review the "William Carey Song" on page 61 (5 minutes).
2. Learn about the Good Character Quality of William on pages 62–64 (10 minutes) and sing the Character Song "We'll Show Diligence" on page 65 (5 minutes).
3. Do the Character Activity for William on page 66 (10 minutes).

William Carey: 45-minute Class

1. Review the "William Carey Song" on page 61 (5 minutes).
2. Review the Character Song "We'll Show Diligence" on page 65 (5 minutes).
3. Do the Shoebox Activity on pages 67 and 68 (10 minutes).
4. Make the Scrimshaw craft on page 69 (15 minutes).
5. Color the map and flag of England on pages 70 and 71 (10 minutes).
   Optional: While the children are coloring, play the "William Carey Song," "We'll Show Diligence," and "I Will Follow" from the companion CD for them to listen to.

Week 9

Amy Carmichael: 30-minute Class

1. Reread the book *Amy Carmichael: Rescuing the Children.* Tell the children to listen carefully because there will be a short quiz afterward (10 minutes).
2. Take the Amy Carmichael Quiz on page 21 (5 minutes).
3. Learn and sing the "Amy Carmichael Song" by listening to the companion CD and following along on page 9 (5 minutes).
4. Color the Amy Carmichael picture on page 7 (10 minutes).
   Optional: While the children are coloring, play the "Amy Carmichael Song," "We'll Show Kindness," and "I Will Follow" from the companion CD for them to listen to.

Amy Carmichael: 45-minute Class

1. Reread the book *Amy Carmichael: Rescuing the Children.* Tell the children to listen carefully because there will be a crossword puzzle afterward (10 minutes).

2. Work the Crossword Puzzle on page 23 (10 minutes).

   Please note: For very young children, sing the "Amy Carmichael Song" on page 9 and "We'll Show Kindness" on page 13 instead of working the crossword puzzle.

3. Read Fascinating Facts About India and Elephants of India on page 17 (5 minutes).

4. Color the Elephants of India on page 18 and the Amy Carmichael picture on page 7 (15 minutes).

   Optional: While the children are coloring, play the "Amy Carmichael Song," "We'll Show Kindness," and "I Will Follow" from the companion CD for them to listen to

5. Review the Prayer Song "I Will Follow" on page 79 (5 minutes).

Week 10

Corrie ten Boom: 30-minute Class

1. Reread the book *Corrie ten Boom: Shining in the Darkness*. Tell the children to listen carefully because there will be a crossword puzzle afterward (10 minutes).

   Please note: For very young children, sing the "Corrie ten Boom Song" on page 27, "We'll Be Brave and Strong" on page 31, and "I Will Follow" on page 79 instead of working the crossword puzzle.

2. Work the Crossword Puzzle on page 42 (10 minutes).

3. Color the Corrie ten Boom picture on page 25 (10 minutes).

   Optional: While the children are coloring, play the "Corrie ten Boom Song," "We'll Be Brave and Strong," and "I Will Follow" from the companion CD for them to listen to.

Corrie ten Boom: 45-minute Class

1. Reread the book *Corrie ten Boom: Shining in the Darkness*. Tell the children to listen carefully because there will be a crossword puzzle afterward (10 minutes).

   Please note: For very young children, sing the "Corrie ten Boom Song" on page 27, "We'll Be Brave and Strong" on page 31, and "I Will Follow" on page 79 instead of working the crossword puzzle.

2. Work the Crossword Puzzle on page 42 (10 minutes).

3. Do the Tulip craft on pages 36 and 37 (15 minutes).

4. Color the Corrie ten Boom picture on page 25 (10 minutes).

   Optional: While the children are coloring, play the "Corrie ten Boom Song," "We'll Be Brave and Strong," and "I Will Follow" from the companion CD for them to listen to.

Week 11

Mary Slessor: 30-minute Class

1. Reread the book *Mary Slessor: Courage in Africa* (10 minutes).

2. Do the Shoebox Activity on pages 51 and 52 (10 minutes).

3. Color the Mary Slessor picture on page 43 (10 minutes).

   Optional: While the children are coloring, play the "Mary Slessor Song," "We'll Be Peacemakers," and "I Will Follow" from the companion CD for them to listen to.

Mary Slessor: 45-minute Class

1. Reread the book *Mary Slessor: Courage in Africa* (10 minutes).
2. Review the "Mary Slessor Song" on page 45 (5 minutes).
3. Make the African Musical Instrument on page 53 (20 minutes).
4. Color the Mary Slessor picture on page 53 (10 minutes).
   Optional: While the children are coloring, play the "Mary Slessor Song," "We'll Be Peacemakers," and "I Will Follow" from the companion CD for them to listen to.

Week 12

William Carey: 30-minute Class

1. Reread the book *William Carey: Bearer of Good News*. Tell the children to listen carefully because there will be a crossword puzzle afterward (10 minutes).
2. Work the Crossword Puzzle on page 74 (10 minutes).
   Please note: For very young children, sing the "William Carey Song" on page 61, "We'll Show Diligence" on page 65, and learn and sing the "Can You Name the Hero?" song on page 75 instead of working the crossword puzzle.
3. Color the William Carey picture on page 59 (10 minutes).
   Optional: While the children are coloring, play the "William Carey Song," "We'll Show Diligence," and "I Will Follow" from the companion CD for them to listen to.

William Carey: 45-minute Class

1. Reread the book *William Carey: Bearer of Good News*. Tell the children to listen carefully because there will be a crossword puzzle afterward (10 minutes).
2. Work the Crossword Puzzle on page 74 (10 minutes).
   Please note: For very young children, sing the "William Carey Song" on page 61, "We'll Show Diligence" on page 65, and "I Will Follow" on page 79 instead of working the crossword puzzle.
3. Do Fun with Rhyme on page 73 (5 minutes).
4. Learn and sing the "Can You Name the Hero?" song by listening to the companion CD and following along on page 75 (5 minutes).
5. Color the William Carey picture on page 59 (10 minutes).
   Optional: While the children are coloring, play the "William Carey Song," "We'll Show Diligence," and "I Will Follow" from the companion CD for them to listen to.
6. Review the Prayer Song "I Will Follow" on page 79 (5 minutes).

Week 13

30-minute Class

1. Sing the "Can You Name the Hero?" song by listening to the companion CD and following along on page 75 (5 minutes).

2. Read the definitions of the character traits on each of the Good Character Quality pages and see if the children can guess the trait and the name of the hero that the trait applies to (5 minutes).

3. Play the game "Who Am I?" Have each child pick the name of one of the four heroes from a basket and give a clue about who that hero is. Let the rest of the class try to guess who the hero is (10 minutes).

4. Have each child pick the name of one of the four heroes from a basket and draw a picture that makes others think of that hero, e.g., a Bible, jungle, or tulip (10 minutes).

45-minute Class

1. Review the "Can You Name the Hero?" song on page 75 (5 minutes).

2. Read the definitions of the character traits on each of the Good Character Quality pages and see if the children can guess the trait and the name of the hero that the trait applies to (5 minutes).

3. Play the game "Who Am I?" Have each child pick the name of one of the four heroes from a basket and give a clue about who that hero is. Let the rest of the class try to guess who the hero is (10 minutes).

4. Have each child pick the name of one of the four heroes from a basket and draw a picture that makes others think of that hero, e.g., a Bible, jungle, or tulip (10 minutes).

5. Tell who your favorite hero is and why (5 minutes).

6. Ask the children to pick their favorite songs and sing them (10 minutes).

Heroes for Young Readers

Written by Renee Taft Meloche • Illustrated by Bryan Pollard

Don't miss the exciting stories of other Christian heroes! Whether reading for themselves or being read to, children love the captivating rhyming text and unforgettable color illustrations of the Heroes for Young Readers series. See the next page for more activity guides and CDs.

BOOKS 1–4

Gladys Aylward: Daring to Trust • Trust in God enabled Gladys Aylward (1902–1970) to safely lead nearly one hundred Chinese orphans on a daring journey that saved their lives. ISBN 1-57658-228-0

Nate Saint: Heavenbound • Nate Saint (1923–1956) flew his plane over the jungles of Ecuador, helping missionaries reach isolated Indians with God's great love. ISBN 1-57658-229-9

Eric Liddell: Running for a Higher Prize • From winning Olympic gold as a runner to leaving his fame in Scotland behind to go to China as a missionary, Eric Liddell (1902–1945) put God in first place. ISBN 1-57658-230-2

George Müller: Faith to Feed Ten Thousand • George Müller (1805–1898) opened an orphanage, trusting God to faithfully provide for the needs of thousands of England's orphaned children. ISBN 1-57658-232-9

BOOKS 5–8

Corrie ten Boom: Shining in the Darkness • Corrie ten Boom (1892–1983) and her family risked everything to extend God's hand of love and protection to their Jewish neighbors during WWII. ISBN 1-57658-231-0

Amy Carmichael: Rescuing the Children • Amy Carmichael (1867–1951) rescued hundreds of women and children, first in Irish slums and then in India, by fearing God and nothing else. ISBN 1-57658-233-7

Mary Slessor: Courage in Africa • Mary Slessor (1848–1915) courageously shared Jesus' life and freedom with the unreached tribes of Africa's Calabar region. ISBN 1-57658-237-X

William Carey: Bearer of Good News • William Carey (1761–1834) left England behind and sailed to faraway India, where he devoted himself to translating the Bible into the native languages. ISBN 1-57658-236-1

BOOKS 9–12

Hudson Taylor: Friend of China • Known as one of the greatest pioneer missionaries of all time, Hudson Taylor (1832–1905) overcame huge obstacles to reach the Chinese. ISBN 1-57658-234-5

David Livingstone: Courageous Explorer • Trailblazing explorer David Livingstone (1813–1873) would not let anything stand in his way as he mapped unexplored Africa and healed the sick. ISBN 1-57658-238-8

Adoniram Judson: A Grand Purpose • Even imprisonment could not stop America's first foreign missionary, Adoniram Judson (1788–1850), as he translated the Bible into Burmese. ISBN 1-57658-240-X

Betty Greene: Flying High • Betty Greene (1920–1997) combined her love of flying with her love for Christ by helping found the Mission Aviation Fellowship. ISBN 1-57658-239-6

BOOKS 13–16

Lottie Moon: A Generous Offering • As a missionary to some of the poorest cities in China, once-wealthy Lottie Moon (1840–1912) experienced having nothing to eat. In dire circumstances, Lottie's first priority was teaching others about God's love. ISBN 1-57658-243-4

Jim Elliot: A Light for God • Jim Elliot (1927–1956) bravely faced both the wonders and the dangers of the South American jungle to share God's love with the feared and isolated Auca people. ISBN 1-57658-235-3

Jonathan Goforth: Never Give Up • In faraway China, despite danger and ridicule, Jonathan Goforth (1859–1936) and his wife generously opened their home to thousands of Chinese visitors, sharing the Good News of the gospel. ISBN 1-57658-242-6

Cameron Townsend: Planting God's Word • After planting God's Word in the hearts of people all over Guatemala and Mexico, Cameron Townsend (1896–1982) started Wycliffe Bible Translators so that all people could read the Good News for themselves. ISBN 1-57658-241-8

For a free catalog of books and materials contact
YWAM Publishing, P.O. Box 55787, Seattle, WA 98155
1-800-922-2143, www.ywampublishing.com

Heroes for Young Readers Activity Guides and CDs

by Renee Taft Meloche

Whether for home, school, or Sunday school, don't miss these fun-filled activity guides and CDs presenting the lives of other Heroes for Young Readers.

Heroes for Young Readers Activity Guides

For Books 1–4: Gladys Aylward, Nate Saint, Eric Liddell, George Müller • 1-57658-367-8
For Books 5–8: Amy Carmichael, Corrie ten Boom, Mary Slessor, William Carey • 1-57658-368-6
For Books 9–12: Betty Greene, David Livingstone, Adoniram Judson, Hudson Taylor • 1-57658-369-4

Heroes for Young Readers Activity Audio CD

Each activity guide has an available audio CD with book readings, songs, and fun activity tracks, helping you to get the most out of the Activity Guides!

CD for Books 1–4 • 1-57658-396-1
CD for Books 5–8 • 1-57658-397-X
CD for Books 9–12 • 1-57658-398-8

Heroes for Young Readers Activity Guide Package Special

Includes the activity guide, audio CD, and four corresponding Heroes for Young Readers hardcover books.

For Books 1–4 Package • 1-57658-375-9
For Books 5–8 Package • 1-57658-376-7
For Books 9–12 Package • 1-57658-377-5

Christian Heroes: Then & Now

by Janet and Geoff Benge

The Heroes for Young Readers books are based on the Christian Heroes: Then & Now biographies by Janet and Geoff Benge. Discover these exciting, true adventures for ages ten and up! Many unit study curriculum guides for older students are also available to accompany these biographies.

Gladys Aylward: The Adventure of a Lifetime • 1-57658-019-9
Nate Saint: On a Wing and a Prayer • 1-57658-017-2
Hudson Taylor: Deep in the Heart of China • 1-57658-016-4
Amy Carmichael: Rescuer of Precious Gems • 1-57658-018-0
Eric Liddell: Something Greater Than Gold • 1-57658-137-3
Corrie ten Boom: Keeper of the Angels' Den • 1-57658-136-5
William Carey: Obliged to Go • 1-57658-147-0
George Müller: The Guardian of Bristol's Orphans • 1-57658-145-4
Jim Elliot: One Great Purpose • 1-57658-146-2
Mary Slessor: Forward into Calabar • 1-57658-148-9
David Livingstone: Africa's Trailblazer • 1-57658-153-5
Betty Greene: Wings to Serve • 1-57658-152-7
Adoniram Judson: Bound for Burma • 1-57658-161-6
Cameron Townsend: Good News in Every Language • 1-57658-164-0
Jonathan Goforth: An Open Door in China • 1-57658-174-8
Lottie Moon: Giving Her All for China • 1-57658-188-8
John Williams: Messenger of Peace • 1-57658-256-6
William Booth: Soup, Soap, and Salvation • 1-57658-258-2
Rowland Bingham: Into Africa's Interior • 1-57658-282-5
Ida Scudder: Healing Bodies, Touching Hearts • 1-57658-285-X
Wilfred Grenfell: Fisher of Men • 1-57658-292-2
Lillian Trasher: The Greatest Wonder in Egypt • 1-57658-305-8
Loren Cunningham: Into All the World • 1-57658-199-3
Florence Young: Mission Accomplished • 1-57658-313-9
Sundar Singh: Footprints Over the Mountains • 1-57658-318-X
C.T. Studd: No Retreat • 1-57658-288-4

For a free catalog of books and materials contact
YWAM Publishing, P.O. Box 55787, Seattle, WA 98155
1-800-922-2143, www.ywampublishing.com